# Trust is everything

Kristina Molloy

BookLeaf Publishing

Presentation by *BookLeaf Publishing*

Web: www.bookleafpub.com

E-mail: info@bookleafpub.com


ISBN: 978-93-95950-25-1

First edition 2022

# Soar with you

Tip toeing to you
A cautious gravitational pull
Not reckless as before
I never was quite the overthinker

Undeserving of this kind of love
Yet here it is
Years in the making holds me steadfast

Frightened to let you in because I know it could
hurt
I've been the victim and the attacker
Show me there is nothing to be afraid of
So I love again and soar with you

# The Piglet

Try to behold the piglet and not the projection
Approach it from a different angle of vision for
deeper understanding
Priceless is knowing what is gifted in faith
The piglet was always there in the mirror

# The end that sets us free

Crawling from the depths of despair
Fighting and searching for a change
Driven by fear; I let you in
I gave and gave; poured myself over
Surfacing buried resentment

Memories cycle like crashing waves
The ocean mist fogs this realty
Our end was the fear
Desperate to hold on
Navigating blindly moving through the seas

Our house was built on a shaky foundation
The shame of keeping this story alive became
my disease
I was always taught to please
Will you ever forgive me one day?

I know the pain is great now
But the freedom to let go is savoury
To taste the freedom we've both been longing
for
The end that sets us free.

# Horizon

Paper plane propels into space
And lands on a sunset dreamscape
Bursting burnt orange beauty!
I ask the horizon, "how did you become this
way?"
She replied "If I told you, my dear, it will take
the mystery away..."

# Mother

5

A fantasy dialogue remains beautiful as an ideal
But there was always something to be said
Of sorrow that dwells deep within
Of a language we could never share

Sighs of exasperation
Nuances of dismissal
Pestering little daughter

Grew up and became a mother to a friend
Mother to a lover
Mother to an enemy
But never mother to herself

Could we ever mend what is broken in an
exchange of words?
Love me, despite my cumbersome nature
Love you, despite the emotional inattentiveness
Infinite words remain unspoken as space
expands us further apart.

# The Nesthead

The enigma of fear
And scary unruly thoughts
As vehemence causes stifle
Grant me the permission to breathe again

A noisy minor bird falls on the nesthead
Shakes the moment of now
As delicate hands detangle and carry the baby
bird
Back up its' moreton bay fig tree home
Catch and release!
All those sticky thoughts too!

# Dreams

It's a craft
A sort of tango of butterflies
Elements of restraint, pace and synchronicity

A confession of the heart escapes your lips
Leaving behind the test of time
Tell me, where is the truth in that?
Let it flow like a steady stream that nourishes all
life that dwells nearby

To find, contain and control, will destroy it
Resuscitate your lost dream
A beckoning feeling compels you so
An outpour of light
The impeding collapse of the mind
Desperation dissipates

Dreams are funny
Ones hold onto dearly with clutching fists
Knuckles going white
Dreams that slowly kill you from within
Break you and leave you completely undone.

Dreams that surprise you
Lacking in fruition

Arrive with reckless abandonment
No planning, no expectations
The dreams that bring forth life

A sanctification of love
The love that existed before you were even born
Before you even realised it was waiting to
explode through all your dream cages
These estranged entanglements holding your
potential to see what was already in front of you

# Inspiration

A kind, gentle embrace
Grace is bestowed in the weakest moments
Rewind, remind and finish with stillness

Solitude reaps spiritual growth
To finally feel the home of the body and the
mind
Canine or feline companions bring rewarding
stewardship
Inspiration is always sought for in the light
Do not forget your birthright
Onlookers seek to leave the darkness
But even the night has the moon and stars

The courage to act overrides resistive thoughts
in due time
Believe in yourself, stand tall and steady, you
strong individual

# Glass

This wired mess needs detangling
Neural pathways to solder and de-solder
Fear and attraction do not belong together
See as the sap begins to bleed from the tree
Resilience to carry onward with the pain and
confusion
Time passes, a dried, russet callous remains
Glass separates us and awaits the shattering
I see you for what you are as I learn more about
myself
Is this what truth feels like?

# Motorcycle

Look ahead to where you wish to go
Help will always be here on the journey
The instructor's tender hand
Guides the pistol grip on the accelerator
"Babes, you're in full graceful control"

Pressure builds in the fingertips
Gradual release of the clutch
Heavy foot on the break eases
Gyroscopic inertia
As the engine purrs

Drive forward and leave the past behind you
The blueprints are engrained into the soul

# Skydive

Three, two, one and lift off
The radome pierces through the atmosphere
Red, yellow, green and exit
Tandem bodies dive and suspend in the air
The adrenaline surge to recalibrate the mind
Is this ultimate brain reset?
An intangible discussion transpires above the
sunny landscape
Thoughts talk to feelings
Feelings ignore thoughts
Instincts override both to align with the moment
Hands maneuver the parachute and spiral
downwards
Feet land heavy and happily on the ground

# Choice

I think of you every single day
I often wonder if you do as well
It pangs me to think
Perhaps, I may not be able to receive
The same kind of love I am willing to give you

I imagined us co-existing without coercion
As we defeat our fears one day at a time
Two tiny homes built on the country side
One for me and one for you
We would give ourselves the space to be
Ignite our bodies at night
To find our ashes in a heap
As dawn light breaks the night sky

Born into a new day of love that heals and
transcends
A shared language that reassures, pleases and
elevates
A sexy whisper in your ear
The taste of your lips on mine
I chose this a thousand times over and over
A choice I could barely resist

# Ana, Justin and Ashleigh

Ana, the favoured one, the Spanish traveller
A tenderness in her eyes and a quietness of her
knowing

Justin, the righteous one, the militia man
A strength in his eyes and the assertiveness of
his stance

Ashleigh, the charcoal tree, the heath consultant
A sensuality in her eyes and the funniness of her
bones

Beautiful people passing on by and I, the
stranger, regard you all.

# Father

Father, I found you amongst the storm of my
shattered mind
For years, I allowed family and religion to
poison me slowly
Unbeknownst, a boundaryless woman ingrained
with harmful habits
Upon your returned phone call tears poured
down my face
October evening stroll through a hot sticky night
Flying termites emerge from a dark spot and
swarm the pathway ahead
Their translucent wings reflecting the amber
lights
Like magical fairies luminating the way, we
follow them to the bridge
A severed connection mended
An exchange of memories that were long stowed
away for this occasion
Healing hearts binding of consolation for you
and me
I gathered the truth in your words as did you in
mine
A glimmer of hope to start again with you

# Jill

My dearest role model
An amazing woman with a strong mind set
She built herself a home and a career to inspire
many
Even mine as chuffed as she is with me
The bee wanted to sting me as I was searching
for a dwelling place
My intentions were pure as I thought about love
and caring for my father
Doubt plays an important parallel to the truth
An accentuating agent that magnifies
How mistaken sometimes we can be about a
person
Father teaches me to keep things to myself now
Especially the scared things that belong solely to
me
I was offended by your turning down but I
understood and respected it
It shifted my trajectory and I can say that I am
happy where I am now
Building a home for myself
Feeling what love is in the own veins
With aspirations to create and inspire others as
well
Just as you did and continue to do so

# Freedom to Fly

17

Fulfilment in a cage is the greatest travesty
Never clip a bird's wings
Freedom to fly, to fail and succeed
The greatest opportunity anyone can ever
experience

# The Cook

Herbed butter cubes ready to fry
Zucchini slices cut to perfection
Jars of condiments topped up and ready for use
The Kingfish, freshly caught this morning
To be served with lemon juice, parsley and
cannellini beans
"Don't forget to add love" barked the Sous chef
Neuroticism fueling their hands
The rush hour begins at six o'clock
Hungry customers waiting to be served
A luxuriously simple dish to concur with their
life conservations
A couple, in the far corner, under the dim light
Sexily gazing into each other eyes, touching
arms softly
A family of five, in the centre, adult children
with their proud parents,
Catching up, smiling and listening intently
A single woman, near the window, open laptop,
Typing manically away, removes her spectacles
and rubs her eyes as she looks at the cook
"Stop daydreaming, you'll burn the fish!" yelled
the Sous Chef

# Tattoo

19

It was only an image but it almost killed me
Heart fluttering ever since
Etched into my mind
Follow the white rabbit home